THEN AND THERE SERIES
GENERAL EDITOR
MARJORIE REEVES

Early Scotland

A. D. CAMERON

Illustrated from contemporary sources

LONGMAN

LONGMAN GROUP LIMITED
Longman House, Burnt Mill, Harlow, Essex CM20 2JE, England
and Associated Companies throughout the World

First published 1986

ISBN 0 582 20092 X

Set in 12/14 pt Linotron Baskerville
Produced by Longman Group (F.E.) Limited.
Printed in Hong Kong

Acknowledgements

I wish to thank the staff of the National Library of Scotland for all their kindness and help and Mr Trevor Cowie of the National Museum of Antiquities who guided me to books and articles on special subjects and answered many questions.

The publishers are grateful to the following for permission to reproduce photographs: BBC, page 50; BBC Hulton Picture Library, page 72; Crown Copyright: reproduced by permission of Historic Buildings and Monuments, Scottish Development Department, pages 17, 18, 24, 45, 52; Cambridge University Collection: copyright reserved, page 53; Department of the Environment, Edinburgh, page 69; Trustees of the National Library of Scotland, pages 22, 66; National Museum of Antiquities of Scotland, pages 5, 11, 33, 35, 55, 62; Royal Commission on Ancient Monuments, Scotland, pages 6, 14, 27, 29, 58, 61; Somerset County Museum, page 39; Alan Sorrell, pages 36, 42. Drawings on pages 44 and 47 from *History for Young Scots. Book 1.* by A.D. Cameron, Oliver and Boyd, 1980.
Cover: Picts carved on a stone at Aberlemno, about AD 750; National Museum of Antiquities of Scotland.

Contents

To the Reader

It is very difficult to find out about the earliest peoples. They could not write and nobody else living at the time could write about them either. We have no way of knowing their names or the language they spoke. We cannot be sure about what they believed, the gods they worshipped, or the great moments in their lives.

Almost the only clues we have about the way they lived are the things they made of pottery and metal and left behind. Other things they made, of wood or cloth or leather, have nearly all rotted away. On good land traces of how they farmed have been wiped out long ago by farmers ploughing and growing crops in the same soil. Many things they lost are still under the ground undiscovered. Some of them must be underneath modern towns. There could be something under your house.

We will never learn everything about the earliest peoples but we are always finding new clues. Trenches cut for oil and gas pipe-lines give a splendid chance to look at what lies under the ground over miles and miles of country. When a bulldozer driver discovers something, he calls in an *archaeologist*, who is an expert on things dug up from early times. The archaeologist will try to *excavate* the whole site, if there is time.

Children sometimes make important discoveries. One boy at St Ninian's Isle in Shetland kept asking some archaeologists if he could help them. They had been digging for three summers inside the ruins of an old church without making very exciting finds. They agreed at last and showed him what to do. On his first day, 4 July 1958, he dug down to a big stone slab. When they lifted it, they found a *hoard* of twenty-eight silver objects.

They were magnificent silver bowls and brooches. Somebody must have hidden them to be safe from *Viking* raiders. They are now known as the St Ninian's Isle Treasure, the greatest find in Scotland in the twentieth century.

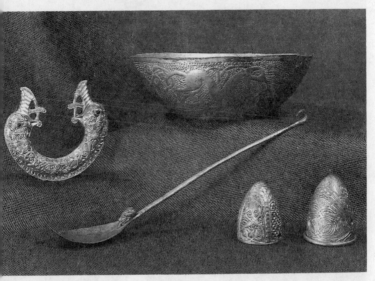

Some of the St Ninian's Isle Treasure, including a bowl and spoon, all finely decorated

Words printed in *italics* are explained in the Glossary on page 76.

Archaeologists uncovering the early Christian graves they found close to the runway of Edinburgh Airport

1 *The Land and the First Visitors*

There was a time long ago when nobody lived in Scotland at all. Imagine we have invented a time machine which makes it possible for us to travel back into the past. Our first journey will be a very long one. We want to go back to about 11,000 years ago. We will find the weather bitterly cold and we will not see any land at all. It is completely hidden under a great sheet of ice, about 1,000 metres thick, just like the land and the sea at the North and South Poles are today. There is no Scotland.

Then the weather became wetter and warmer. The ice began to melt in the sun and turned to water. After a long time the low land in the south appeared and the lower slopes of the hills lost their covering of ice. *Glaciers* and melting water brought down gravel and mud in which plants took root. Animals from warmer parts of Europe could move in to graze on them, because Britain was still joined by land to Europe. Reindeer and horses came first. Birch trees and pine trees began to grow, and in came other kinds of deer, as well as wild boars and wild cattle. This change went on for a long time – about 3,000 years.

There were people in warmer places, such as Spain and the south of France, living in rock shelters or caves. They lived by hunting. We know this from the magnificent pictures artists painted on cave walls of the animals they hunted, some with arrows sticking into them.

Let us take another look for early Scotland by travelling in the time machine to a point some 7,500 years ago. We see that the ice has gone. When it melted it made the sea rise and cover all the lower land. The English Channel has been formed and Britain has been cut off from the rest of Europe. It has become an island. Other pieces of high land, off the west coast of Scotland, have also been cut of to become the islands they are today. Great forests of oak and elm, ash and hazel have taken hold where the soil was good, and pine and birch have spread north or higher up the hills.

By 5500 BC Scotland as a whole had become a land with plants and trees and animals, where it was possible for people to live. But it was still colder than most places, not a place people would rush to in great numbers.

RADIOCARBON DATING

The earliest people in Scotland camped at Morton in Fife which you will see on the map inside the front cover. At that time this was a little island close to the coast. The only clues they left behind are their camp fires and their rubbish. You might think these are things which would rot quite quickly and tell us very little, but archaeologists have a way of finding out how old a camp like this is. They use a method called radiocarbon dating.

In 1949 an American called Walter Libby made an amazing discovery which made it possible to tell almost exactly when these people were at Morton. Libby discovered that all living things, including people, take in from the air around them a special kind of carbon called radiocarbon or *carbon-14*. They all contain the same tiny amount of it. When a tree is cut down, it dies and stops taking in carbon-14. When animals or people die, they

8

stop taking in carbon-14. They begin to decay and instead give off carbon-14. Libby also discovered that as living things decay they all give off carbon-14 at exactly the same rate.

Because scientists know how much carbon-14 something contained when it was alive, they need to test only a small sample in their laboratory to find out how much it has left. This allows them to work out the number of years it has been giving off carbon-14.

The scientist who tested several pieces of *charcoal* from Morton discovered they had been losing carbon-14 for more than 7,000 years. The oldest piece told him that someone had cut down the wood for the first fire there in about 5500 BC. This proves that people were living in Scotland at a very early date, much earlier than scholars believed before Libby made his discovery.

FOOD GATHERERS AND FISHERS IN FIFE

When they were digging at Morton the archaeologists found a fireplace with charcoal and blackened stones round it. They also discovered slight hollows in the sand where people had curled up and slept beside the fire. They think the first people at Morton slept in the open and covered themselves with animal skins to keep warm. Several little stone tools and chips of stone lay scattered about. That is all there is to show that there were people here.

We think that at first there were only a few people at Morton, say three or four, and that they did not stay long, perhaps only a week or two. They must have set off from some place farther south in good weather. They probably came by sea in a boat they had made by chipping out the centre of the trunk of a tree. They must have liked the look

9

of the little island. With water all around, it was safe from wild animals. Yet it was not difficult to cross to the mainland when the tide was out. They could gather shellfish, cockles and big mussels on the shore. And there were fish in the waters, and birds in the marshes and up on the cliffs, and wood for the fire, and berries and nuts to eat.

It is very likely that these people kept coming back each year, and staying longer, and that they brought others with them. Perhaps some of them came to live in Scotland all the time, sometimes on the coast and sometimes inland. One thing is certain because later finds prove it: people went on living on Morton island for hundreds of years.

Later people built themselves a hut to live in. We know that it was long and narrow, because the holes for its wooden posts still show up as a different colour in the soil, and it could have been thatched with reeds from the marsh. In late summer these people would try to catch a lot of fish. They would dry them in the sun for the winter when food was difficult to catch. They could go out in the boat, hoping to catch big cod with a net. Closer inshore, they could use a raft and spear fish with a *harpoon*. This was a spear with barbs to jag into a fish and stop it wriggling away. Archaeologists found bones in their *midden* which prove that they once caught a *sturgeon* which was 3 metres long and must have weighed about 250 kilos. The people must have told the story of that fish for a very long time!

On some days the children would go climbing trees to collect hazelnuts. The men went climbing too – up the cliffs to the west to capture *gannets*. At other times they might hunt in a gang to kill a deer or a wild ox with their *flint*-tipped spears. Then they would have plenty of meat, another skin to make someone something to wear, lots of *sinews* for tying things, and bone or *antler* for making tools.

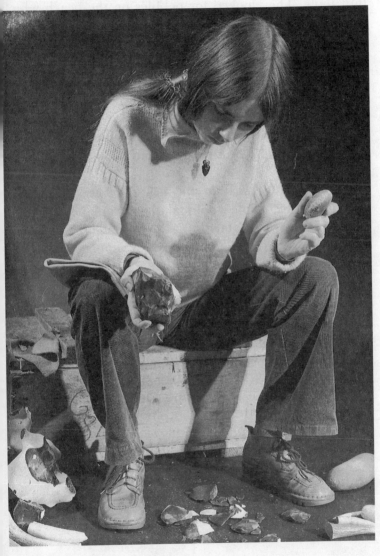

A modern girl making flint tools in the old way

Flint was very scarce in Scotland but the people at Morton could make tools which were nearly as good as flint tools. They looked for pebbles on the beach which were as hard as flint (and which we know as *chert*). If they hit the pebble at the correct angle, using another stone as a hammer, it would split along the grain. Each good flake which broke off could be used as a tool. Long flakes became blades like knives, shorter ones scrapers like chisels, narrow pointed ones borers, called *awls*, for making holes in things. These tools belong to the period called the 'Middle Stone Age', from 5500 to about 3700 BC.

If they came back to the island feeling hungry in springtime the people would take eggs from the cliffs, with the birds screeching and diving down on them. Later on, it would be easy to catch young birds or *moulting* birds out at sea.

At present, Morton island gives us our earliest glimpse of people in Scotland. They were not settlers but people on the move, living on shellfish, or things which moved – animals, birds and fish. They did not know it but a little later on there were other people living the same kind of lives in other parts of the country: in caves near Oban for example, on islands such as Jura and Oronsay, and on the coast of Galloway. We do not know how many people there were in Scotland altogether. It may have been more than fifty, probably not much more than a hundred.

2 Early Farmers

The earliest farmers we know about in Europe came from
the Middle East bringing seeds and animals such as sheep
and goats with them. They moved into Greece, then
slowly into the valley of the Danube where many of them
settled, and on to the great plains of central and western
Europe.

The remains of their settlements in Germany and
Holland show that they lived in villages in large houses
made of wood. Each house was about 30 metres long.
Even if some of the space inside was for the cattle, these
houses were far too big for a modern-sized family. The
people in each house, whoever they were, must have been
friendly enough with each other to be able to live together.
Probably each house was the home of what we call an
extended family – grandparents, their sons and daughters
and their wives and husbands and their grandchildren –
perhaps twenty people all living under the same great
roof.

Perhaps the earliest farmers to come to Britain lived in
big wooden houses too. If you think your own house is not
likely to be standing in a thousand years time, you will
agree that the first wooden houses must have disappeared
long ago. But when nothing can be seen on the ground, the
outlines of early buildings sometimes show up on 13

photographs taken from the air. In the dry summer of 1976 an air photograph over Balbridie Farm in Kincardineshire revealed a shape like the big houses discovered in Europe. The shape was on a ridge which is still being cultivated today, safely above the River Dee. When it was excavated it turned out, as you can see from the picture, to be the burned remains of a huge wooden house. It had been 26 metres long and exactly half as wide, and it must have been nearly 9 metres high. A house with such a wide roof, far wider than the earliest farmhouses in Europe, and built in the far north of Britain, could not be so very old, the excavators thought. It seemed to be more like the

14   *The discovery of the Balbridie house – what the cameraman first saw from the air*

wooden halls the Anglo-Saxons built in the south about AD 500. But radiocarbon tests on the charcoal showed that this house was burned down about 3700 BC. Burned wheat and barley seeds were also found – at this very early date people were already farming in Scotland. We call this the 'New Stone Age' because people could also make good tools of polished stone.

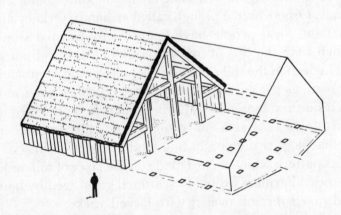

What the Balbridie house probably looked like: compare it with the size of the man

The Balbridie house is a most exciting discovery. It shows that there were settlers in Kincardineshire in very early times and that they were clever people. They had the tools to cut down big oak trees, to shape wood and to join pieces of wood together (remember they had no metal nails). But we do not know who the builders were. They could have been incomers who brought tools in their boats, as well as seeds and animals, when they came over from Europe to the north-east of Scotland. Or they could have been settlers already living in Britain who taught themselves to build this kind of house because it suited their needs. What do you think?

15

FARMING

Early farmers found more grass for their animals in open country than in thick woods. When they needed more land they took their axes of polished stone and cut down bushes and trees. Orkney was a good place for early farmers to live because it was lightly wooded, with only some birch, willow and bushes before 3000 BC. Some people would dig the soil using an ox's shoulder-blade as a spade. Others used a plough called an *ard*. In Orkney and Shetland local people have found many pointed stones which were the tips of this kind of plough. It did not go down deep in the soil or turn it over like a modern plough. Instead, as the oxen pulled it along, it pushed the soil to each side and loosened it. Early farmers first ploughed up and down a patch of ground and then across it. Archaeologists digging in Shetland discovered this criss-cross pattern which an ard made on the layer of soil under the peat. Farmers probably scattered grain seed by hand and raked the soil over it with forked sticks.

LIVING AT SKARA BRAE, 3100-2450 BC

Some early farmers in Orkney were re-discovered after a great storm in 1850. The storm swept away part of a sand dune on the west side on the Bay of Skaill and laid bare the tops of walls in the shape of houses. This was an archaeologist's dream. The sand had hidden the village of Skara Brae from sight for thousands of years but it had preserved it exactly as it once had been. Life in the village had come to an end in another storm long ago. The sand and the sea swept into the houses so quickly that the people had to flee for their lives. In the rush to get out, somebody's necklace snapped and the bone beads were left lying exactly where they fell.

16

The village of Skara Brae where people lived five thousand years ago

The half dozen homes at Skara Brae were all close together and built of stone. There was plenty of good stone, called Caithness flagstone, in flat slabs which were easy to split and easy to break cleanly into blocks of a handy size. The builders gave each house double walls. They built up the walls layer by layer (like a bricklayer today), keeping the walls straight but making the corners curved.

Then they filled in the gap between the inner and outer walls with ashes to keep the house warm. We are just beginning to do the same: we call it insulation. Outside their walls they dumped more rubbish over the years until it sloped right up to the top of the walls. It was possible to crawl from house to house along a covered passage. Each house had one big room and also a little room, probably a lavatory, inside the wall with a drain running from it.

We are not certain what kind of roof the houses had. 17

There was not much wood in Orkney but driftwood all the way from America sometimes came ashore. Wooden rafters could carry a roof made of stone slates, or thatch, or turf. Whalebone could have been used as rafters and a whale's skin would have been the only piece of material big enough to cover a hut. No sign of wood remains but the jaw bones of a whale were found in one hut as if they had fallen down from the roof. Which do you think they used?

They used stones, not wood, to make furniture. Long flat slabs laid on stone supports quickly became the shelves of a dresser to put their pots and bowls on. They even made their beds of stone, but they put heather in them to make them springy and dry grass on top to be soft and comfortable.

Inside one of the houses at Skara Brae: can you see the beds, dresser, fireplace, and the way into the 'little room'?

Early people had to work a long time every day to get the things they needed most – food, shelter and clothing. If they did not, they knew they would die. Let us see what we can find out about how these people fed and clothed themselves. Here is a list of things which archaeologists have discovered in their excavations:

Clues discovered about food	How many?
Bones of cattle, especially younger animals	Commonest animal bones
Bones of sheep and goats	Many
Bones and antlers of red deer	Few
Whale bones	A few stranded whales
Fishbones of cod and coalfish	Thousands
Shells, especially limpets – food or bait?	Thousands
Seabird bones, especially gannets	Some
Cereal grains (and a *saddle quern* for grinding them into flour)	Some

What does this tell you about their usual food?

People cooked their food in pots on the fire. The potter decorated the pots by scratching grooves on the soft clay before it was fired. The grooves might be straight lines side by side, or diamond shapes or *spirals*. The only other place where we find the same patterns on pottery is in the 19 south of England where the great stone circles of Stonehenge and Avebury were built. As we shall soon see stone circles being built in Orkney at this time too, we know for sure where the Skara Brae people came from.

There are no signs that the people in Skara Brae could spin or weave, but they could make clothes out of animal skins. Archaeologists have found flint knives for cutting skins, scrapers for scraping the fat off them, bone borers for making holes in them and bone needles for sewing them together. Clothes made of leather last a long time and sheepskin coats are warm. No wonder many people still wear them!

People did not need beads in the same way as they needed food but they liked to wear them. They made them out of shells by boring holes to string them through. Or they cut hollow bones into lengths and made them smooth. Or a man might hang round his neck some unusual object, something he had to struggle for perhaps, like the tip of a walrus' ivory tusk.

The people at Skara Brae also liked to paint their bodies. Archaeologists discovered little pots of red and white paint in the smaller bed, the woman's, but probably the whole family painted themselves on special occasions.

The dates we have for people living at Skara Brae show that they came early, about 3100 BC and stayed for a long, long time, until 2450 BC. They were crofter-fishermen, making a living on both land and sea. On land the man was a farmer, keeping animals mainly but also growing some grain. At times he had also to be a boat-builder, a hut-repairer or a furniture-maker. A woman's work was in and around the home. She would make flour, bake and cook the meals. She would see to the milking and probably
look after young animals as well as her own children. And

if the men were away, she would have a lot more to do.

Now look back at the picture of Skara Brae on p.17.

Can you imagine these people at home on a stormy night? The hut is dark except for the flicker of the fire on the hearth, the door shut tight to cut down the draught, people in bed early pulling their coverings of skins up over them, a burst of coughing now and then when the wind blows the smoke back into the room. They forget the roar of the wind and the waves outside and fall asleep. For them there will be another day.

3   Great Builders with Big Stones

The drawing on this page of standing stones in Orkney was made by a minister over 200 years ago. It is interesting that the Christian church *A* had been built so close to the Stones of Stenness *C* where people had worshipped in earlier times, long before Christianity came to Scotland. In the 1700s people called these stones 'the temple of the moon' and in the picture we see what it meant in their lives. The girl is on her knees inside the standing stones asking the god Odin to help her keep her promises to the young man beside her. Over the bridge is a more complete circle at *F*, the Ring of Brodgar. This was 'the temple of the sun', where the young man in his turn

would pray in front of the girl. Then at *D*, 'the standing stone with the hole in the middle', the two young people clasp hands through the hole and promise to be true to each other. Good Christians though they were, this was still a very sacred promise to them.

Not everything these people believed was true, of course. They said *B* in the picture was 'just a mound raised up for archers to shoot at'. It had not been opened then and they did not know that it was Maes Howe (see p. 24), a splendid *chambered tomb* built earlier than the Pyramids of Egypt. They also connected the stone circles with Thor and Odin – who were gods to the Vikings much later. Over the centuries different peoples have all looked on the stone circles as holy places.

Is it possible for us at this late date to find out who built the stone circles in the picture, and why they built them, and how?

The stone houses and stone furniture at Skara Brae (see Chapter 2) prove that the people there were good at building. Maes Howe and the stone circles in the picture are no more than 10 kilometres away, and radiocarbon tests have shown that they were put up at the same time. It is almost certain that Skara Brae people helped to build them. Although more villages have not yet been found on the mainland of Orkney, this was the kind of place where a large number of people could have lived. Maes Howe is so huge that whoever wanted to build it must have been someone who had power over lots of poorer families and made them come and work for him. It must be the burial place of the family of a great chief.

INSIDE MAES HOWE

You can go inside Maes Howe if you keep your head   23

down. It is dark as you feel your way in. The floor, the walls, the roof are great slabs of stone. Inside you are in a big central room with plenty of space. The walls, as you can see in the picture below, are built up of flat slabs laid one on top of the other, and look like piles of massive books. They fit so exactly that there is hardly room to force the blade of a knife between them. The slabs above your head overhang each other to form a *vault*. In three cells, like the one in the picture, there was room to lay the bodies of the dead, and at certain times of the year people came inside to worship.

Inside Maes Howe. The two upright stones are far taller than a man

Was there ever treasure in here? Adventurers always expect to find gold and silver under a big green mound like this but Maes Howe was built before these precious metals were discovered. Probably there never was any treasure, but thousands of years later Vikings broke in, hoping they would find some. One of the Vikings took his axe and sadly scratched the message that the treasure had been carried off before they arrived!

PEOPLE, SUN AND GODS

There must have been a few people in Early Britain who were *astronomers*, who understood the movements of the sun and the moon and could make a reliable calendar. We know this best from the stone circle at Stonehenge in the south of Britain. If you stand in the centre of the circle, early on 21 June, you will find a single standing stone, called the Heel Stone, marks exactly the point on the horizon where the sun comes up and this tells you that it is midsummer's day. The Clava Cairns near Inverness are tombs surrounded by stone circles. Exactly as the sun goes down on midwinter afternoon, it is shining straight along the entrance passages and into the tombs. Were the Cairns built at this angle to let in the sun to awaken or warm the spirits of the dead? From another great stone circle at Callanish on the Isle of Lewis (see the picture on the next page), rows of stones run off, one due south, another due west. This proves that these people also knew the *cardinal points* of the compass.

People used to meet inside the ring of tall stones at Brodgar for ceremonies to help them in their lives. They must have been frightened of many things: sickness, which might kill their children or animals, too little rain for their crops, or too much. Every flash of lightning, every

25

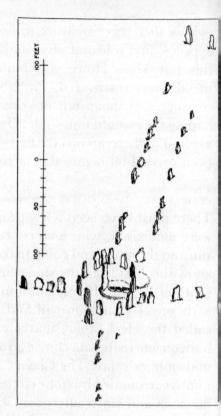

The circle and rows of standing stones at Callanish on the Isle of Lewis

rumble of thunder, every sudden storm were signs to them that the gods could be very angry. Like African tribes or Red Indians, they probably had a witch-doctor or a medicine-man to lead them, specially dressed up with his body all decorated with paint. With his help they would try to please the gods and then the sun would come out and warm Mother Earth and give them good crops and food in plenty.

The Ring of Brodgar was their 'temple of the sun'. They came there in the early hours of midsummer's day, when it is never really dark in Orkney, and waited for the big red face of the sun to show itself. The medicine-man told them this was going to be the longest day. Their festival in midwinter (on 21 December, not far away from our Christmas) was very different. That day was short and cold but they were promised that the sun would come back a little longer each day to give more light and keep them warm.

They probably had other festivals: in spring when they sowed the seed, in early May when cows and young calves went out to new pastures, and at harvest-time. Then at the end of October (our Hallowe'en) they lit fires to fight the darkness that was coming. People would join in, singing, stamping their feet to the beat of the drum, dancing round the fire and in and out of the standing stones. The noise and the excitement mounted. Human skulls from the tombs, held high on tall poles in the centre, were signs that their ancestors were with them. The medicine-man took things which the people valued and offered them up to the gods. He might take a fine clay pot and smash it with a stone axe, to show how much they were willing to give up. Or he would take an animal which had just been killed and place it on the central fire. These offerings were *sacrifices* to please the gods.

LAYING OUT THE RING OF BRODGAR

The stones of the Ring at Brodgar are huge. Each weighs about 2 tonnes. We call them *megaliths* which means 'very large stones'. Recently the 400 circles of standing stones in Scotland were measured and it was discovered that the builders had been using a unit of measurement of their own, equal to 2 feet 8⅔ inches (0.83 metre). This measurement is now known as the *megalithic yard [MY]*, and is very close to the length of a man's pace. Using it to 27 mark out the length of anything is easy – you decide on the number of paces and count as you walk!

The megalithic yard is also the average length from a man's cupped hand when he stretches out his arm sideways, to the tip of his nose. As you can see from the diagram below, if two men reach out an arm towards each other and clasp hands the distance between their noses will be 2 MY.

If several men form a circle with their arms stretched out and hold hands they will all be on the *circumference*, or outside edge, of the circle and the same distance [2 MY] apart.

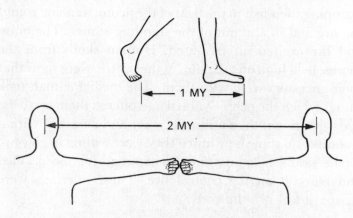

THE *diameter* of the Ring of Brodgar is exactly 125 MY. Its *radius* is half of that, 62½ MY. Can you imagine how the men from Skara Brae and all around might have been called to the chosen spot to help the stone circle to take shape? Try to work out how the Ring of Brodgar, which has sixty stones in it, was laid out.

The Ring of Brodgar is not the only circle in the British Isles which is this size. Avebury in the south of England has two stone circles which are exactly the same diameter

(125 MY) and New Grange in the east of Ireland has one, which is probably the earliest of them all.

MOVING THE STONES

In a quarry 11 kilometres north-west of the Ring of Brodgar some big stone slabs are today still lying ready to be moved. They are the same rock and the same size as the stones in the Ring of Brodgar. This is where the standing stones are likely to have come from, but how? They were too heavy to carry. They could have been dragged all the way with ropes by a large number of men. Or they could have been dragged 4 kilometres to the edge of the Loch of

The sun shining on standing stones in the Ring of Brodgar in Orkney

Harray and taken the rest of the way by water. Three or four men could have paddled a stone across quite easily on canoes which had been lashed together. That is probably how the famous blue stones from West Wales travelled most of the way to Stonehenge, 240 kilometres away. But how did they raise such big stones?

First they dug a hole bigger than the base of the stone which was to go in it. The back of the hole was straight but on the inside it sloped from ground level down to the bottom. The stone to be raised rested on two logs. When they pushed it forward, it tilted gently down the slope into the hole.

With a lot of tall stones to set up, however, they probably used a pair of *sheerlegs*. A rope from the top of them went round the top of the stone. Teams of men hauled on the ropes and slowly the sheerlegs and the stone came up towards them. As soon as the stone was upright, a shout went up, 'Hold!'. Big *chocking-stones* were slipped in on the sloping side, packing stones at the back and sides, and the hole was filled in. One up, fifty-nine to go!

Then they dug a deep ditch all round, leaving only two entrances to the circle. The ditch was so big that it would have taken forty men a whole year to dig if they had been working full time. It cut the Ring off from the world outside. The Ring of Brodgar was now their special place.

4 Traders, Incomers and Makers of Things

TRADERS

Before there were any roads, carrying goods overland was not easy. You had to carry them on your back or on somebody else's. Taking cargoes in a boat was much easier. People traded by sailing close to the coast and up sea-lochs and rivers. Stone axes found round the Firth of Clyde prove that some traders must also have come across the sea from Ireland in their little boats. The axes are a special kind of stone found in quarries in northern Ireland. Stone axes did not take up much room in a boat and were quite valuable. The traders probably came over after the farmers had the harvest in and so had some corn to spare to offer in exchange. A fine polished axe with a sharp blade cost a lot of grain: poorer men bought rough axes and made them smooth themselves. They did not yet use money.

Many Irish axes have also been found in the north-east, in Aberdeenshire. These axes prove that people who lived quite far apart sometimes met each other to trade.

POTTERS

Clay pots break easily. People on the move, like the hunters and fishers at Morton in Fife whom you read about in Chapter 1, did not have any. They put things in the bladders of animals, or nets, or bags made of leather. People with clay pots live in a settled home.

A potter probably worked on a turntable. He or she would lay one ring of clay on top of another, smoothing away the joins with wet fingers. Then the pot would be heated in the ashes of a fire or in a hot *kiln* to make it hard.

Pots come in different shapes and sizes. Big pots were usually for storing things in, expecially corn. Smaller, stout pots were cooking pots. Flat shallow bowls were probably for milk, to let it settle for making cheese or butter. Round-bottomed pots stand quite well on rough floors but at Skara Brae, where people had flat shelves to stand pots on, their pots had flat bottoms as well.

INCOMERS

We find much finer drinking cups, called *beakers*, appearing in Scotland in large numbers from about 2300 BC. You can see one on page 35. We simply call the people who brought them the Beaker people. They must have come across to Scotland from the mouth of the Rhine in Holland because the same cups are found in both places.

These Beaker people were rich and powerful. Their chiefs liked to carry well-made weapons and to wear fine ornaments. Beaker people did not bury a number of bodies together in one great tomb like Maes Howe but singly in short stone boxes called *cists*. They laid the body on its side in a crouched position, with the knees tucked up under the chin. Often a beaker was placed beside the body inside the cist.

They buried fine things with their dead. Some of the Beaker women may be described as 'the gold set'. They liked crescent necklaces, like the one in the picture, cut out of sheet gold, thin and very fine. One woman in

Morayshire also had gold ear-rings. They were shaped like a long basket, over 10cm long, using gold from the

A modern girl wearing a crescent and a long earring of sheet gold, which belonged to the Beaker people

Wicklow mountains in Ireland and probably made by an Irish goldsmith. Other women, 'the jet set', were wearing fine necklaces made of beads of polished *jet*. The black beads in three rows were spread out to make the shape of a crescent as well. Some of the women had jet bracelets and jet buttons on their clothes.

The things Beaker people put in a grave, like those in the picture opposite, give us some hints about their ideas on life after death. Was the beaker itself filled with a drink like beer for a journey? Was a flint *strike-a-light* put in in case the dead man wanted to make a fire? Would he need his flint arrowheads when he was out hunting for food? Did they believe that he really needed his wristguard – to protect his arm against the 'kick' from the string of his bow? Or were these things to tell the gods how important this man was? All of them were discovered in a short cist at Culduthel near Inverness in 1975.

Four little studs in the man's wristguard were made of copper capped with gold. Like the gold crescents the women wore, they are proof that with the Beaker people we have arrived in an Age of Metals.

METAL WORKERS

In the middle of Europe, Beaker people were already making things of copper and gold. If they came to the British Isles looking for metals, they certainly found them, especially in Ireland. In Scotland they discovered copper in Galloway, Ayrshire, Lanarkshire and Argyll, and gold in the Border hills, Perthshire and in the far north in Sutherland.

Copper is a soft metal. A smith can melt it by heating it and he can pour it into a *mould* of stone or clay hollowed out to the shape he wants. The mould the smith in the

Found in a Beaker grave near Inverness: a beaker and (clockwise) a belt buckle, an amber bead, flint arrowheads, a strike-a-light, and wristguard

picture on page 36 is using is the shape of an axe. This is called casting. Then if the smith hits the axehead with a hammer he will make it harder and give it a sharper edge. But a copper axe is too soft to stay sharp for long.

Some of the early people – we do not know who – discovered that you can make copper harder by adding to it a little, say 5 per cent to 10 per cent, of another soft metal, tin. This mixture of copper and tin is called *bronze* and the period when it was used in Britain for making the best tools and weapons is known as the 'Bronze Age', which lasted from 2000 to 600 BC.

There was tin in only one part of Britain, however, in Cornwall. Therefore every bronze axe, every bronze knife, dagger, chisel, sword, spearhead and ornament a bronze-smith made anywhere in Britain must have had in it some Cornish tin. Places where moulds have been found prove that many bronzesmiths had to get their copper and tin from far away. Probably the most distant of all was the bronzesmith in the eighth century BC at Jarlshof in Shetland, which is about 1,600 kilometres away from Cornwall. Traders followed well-known sea routes, some carrying copper in lumps called *ingots*, some carrying tin, and all selling the tools and weapons the bronzesmiths made.

The first bronze axes looked just like flat stone axes. Then the blade was made wider than was possible in stone. The axehead fitted into a hole in the wooden *haft*, or handle, and had to be tied to it with strips of leather. The second axe here ensures a better fit. It fits into a V cut in

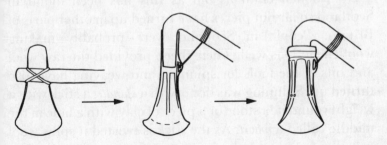

37

the end of a crooked haft which is held tightly by *flanges* on the side of the axehead and a ridge across the middle. Again the axe head is tied and has a special hole for the cord to pass through. The third kind of axehead is hollow at the top: the haft fits into it instead of the axe fitting into the handle.

Beaker people had other bronze weapons, such as daggers and spears, but these do not prove that in the Bronze Age people were always fighting. The same weapons were just as useful for hunting. Two of them, the dagger and the axe, are also tools. A man might cut up meat with his dagger to eat it, and chop down trees with his axe. Many forests were cleared to give space for farming at this time.

CLOTH MAKERS

In 1963 a man ploughing near Dundee made an interesting find. His plough turned up one bronze spearhead and two bronze swords. Inside the socket of the spearhead a small piece of cloth was discovered. It had probably been wrapped round the tip of the shaft to make a tight fit. The cloth is linen, which is made from *flax*. The weapons belong to the late Bronze Age and make the cloth eighth century BC in date. This shows that people were making linen in Scotland 2,700 years ago.

No woollen cloth as old as this has been found in Scotland so far but pieces have turned up in other parts of Britain. People in Scotland were probably making woollen cloth as well. Their sheep provided the raw wool and bits of the tools for spinning and weaving have also turned up. Spinning was done with a *spindle*, a stick with a weight round it, a stone or a piece of clay with a hole in the middle called a *whorl*. As the stick is twisted it spins wool

38

into *yarn* for weaving. Early people used to weave on a *loom* like the one in the picture below. You can see the up and down threads, the *warp*, have stone weights tied on to keep them tight. The weaver raises every odd warp thread, the first, the third, the fifth and so on, and lowers every even thread, the second, fourth, etc., then she can pass the *weft* straight through between them. When she changes over the warp threads she has the dark weft thread locked in position and she pushes it against the woven cloth at the top with her bone comb. She is now ready to pass the weft thread back to the other side.

Both spinning and weaving seem to have been jobs done by women. A picture of a spinner and a weaver as early as this exists, scratched on a pot found in Central Europe. They are both women.

A model showing what an early loom looked like

5 Forts, Crannogs and Brochs

Until about 1000 BC the weather was warmer and drier than now and very good for growing crops. Farmers could grow corn as high up as 300 metres then. In one high place we know about, Green Knowe in Peeblesshire, they cut into the slope and used the soil they dug out to make a row of nine platforms. On each one they built a round house, with a wall of *wattle and daub*. About forty to fifty people must have lived here without feeling any need to build a wall all round to protect themselves. Probably they had cut down trees and bushes to provide grazing for more animals but querns for grinding corn which were found prove that they were also growing grain. With more meat and grain to eat, more people could be kept alive in Scotland and the population rose.

About 1000 BC however, more rain began to fall and the weather became colder. From about 600 BC it became wetter and colder still. People had to stop trying to grow crops on such high ground. Others were forced out of farms on low land because a blanket of peat gradually spread over fertile soil. In Shetland archaeologists have found under the peat the outlines of farm buildings and fields with stone *dikes* round them which people had built earlier in the Bronze Age. Suddenly, it seems, good land was becoming scarce. In Jarlshof, once a comfortable

40

place to live on the coast of Shetland, a bronzesmith came to work. His clay moulds show that he was making slashing swords, and other smiths were making lots of swords in other parts of Scotland. This is a sign that farmers needed swords to defend themselves against hungry men who would kill them to gain land. Where people lived on hill-tops they dug ditches and built *ramparts* with stone walls on top to keep their families and their animals safe.

Finavon in Angus is a good example of a fort built on top of a hill. Thanks to radio-carbon dating, we know that it was built before 600 BC. Perhaps the farmers beside this hill had not yet been attacked, but they had heard stories about others who had. They decided that the top of the hill (200 metres high) was the safest place to live. If they built a wall all round it and made it really stout no one would dare attack them.

You can see them at work in the picture on page 42. Their fort was going to have two long parallel sides and be curved at each end. The wall round it was to be very thick, six metres thick. First they had to gather all the materials they needed. One gang of men with hammers and wedges were in the quarry cutting sandstone into blocks. Women, boys and girls worked with the men in the transport gang. They carried big stones and baskets of little stones and dumped them in heaps near where the wall was to be. Other men were cutting down the trees nearest the fort. They wanted straight trunks as long as the width of the wall and up to 30 cm thick. Lighter branches would be handy for the houses they would build inside, up against the walls.

They had started building on the outside of the fort lower down the hill and laid the biggest stones on the bare   41

A modern artist's idea of how a hill-top fort was built

soil. They built it up to the level of the inside and piled in smaller stones and earth. A wall like this built up to a great height without *mortar*, however, would fall down. Like the human body it needed a skeleton to support it. The fort-builders knew this. You can see them laying tree trunks at intervals across the wall as it rose higher with lighter timbers to connect them to each other. When it was complete, an enemy would see a wall three times the height of any man.

Finavon's walls have been *vitrified*. This means that they have been burned at such a great heat (over 1000°C) that the stones in them melted and joined together in a solid mass. When the logs between the stones burned they left spaces, which acted as *flues*. The wind rushing through them might force the fire up to this tremendous heat. Might the fort-dwellers have burned the walls themselves deliberately to make them solid?

In an experiment in a television programme in 1980 a team tried to find out. They built a timber-laced wall like these people did. Then they piled lots of branches and twigs against the wall and set them alight. The blaze set the wood in the wall on fire and it burned until gaps could be clearly seen between the stones. Stones cracked but when the team looked for signs of rocks melting and sticking to each other on cooling, they found only two small pieces. Not much to show for all their work! Probably their fire had not been hot enough. Possibly they had not chosen a day with great gusts of wind.

Did the fort-dwellers really try to burn their walls themselves? Or did an enemy burn them? We still do not know for certain. What do you think?

Because the houses were built of wood and leant against the inside of the wall, the risk of them going on fire was always high. If a house caught fire accidentally on a very windy day the wind would whip the flames through the roofs and walls of other houses and set the wall itself ablaze. It would probably have burned homes, walls, everything and been a sad day for the people in the fort.

Later on, however, several of the vitrified forts became places to live in again. Craig Phadrig near Inverness is an example: it burned about 400 BC and had people living in t about AD 600, at the time of the Picts (see Chapter 7).

CRANNOGS

In the south-west of Scotland particularly, people looked for safety on islands. Water all round them made them safe from wild animals and robbers. The island in Milton Loch in Galloway is not a natural island at all. About 500 BC people made it and built a house on it. This kind of island home is called a crannog.

They chose a shallow place not too far from the land. They had to take out boat-loads of stones and dump them on the spot until their island began to show its shape above the water. Then they placed large logs side by side in a layer, with other layers on top to raise the floor safely above the water. The main timbers of the house, such as the door posts, were held upright because they fitted exactly into square holes specially cut in logs in the floor. With wooden walls and a thatched roof, this round house contained several rooms. In one the people had their fire on a clay hearth surrounded by stones and the smoke

Underwater causeway ————

The crannog in Milton Loch

found its way out through a hole in the roof. Outside they could walk right round on a wide wooden platform. On the side away from the shore they made a little harbour, a sheltered place for their boats. Connecting the crannog with the shore was a *causeway*, or pathway, which ran zig-zag below the surface of the water. The children in the crannog knew well the way it went: a stranger in a hurry might fall into deeper waters!

44

The people often caught birds which fed in the loch. They were also in a good position to catch fish. Much of their food, however, came from the land. Two objects found in the crannog prove this. One was a quern for grinding grain; the other was a wooden plough, one of the earliest to be found in Scotland.

BROCHS

Later, in the first century BC, people called Celts came and built a new and exciting kind of stronghold. This was the round stone tower you can see below, which we call a *broch*. There were five hundred of them in the north-west and the north, on the islands and the mainland of Scotland, but in other countries there were none at all.

The Broch of Mousa as it is today

Let us imagine we can go back and visit the people in a broch. The old warrior we meet outside tells us, 'My people built them. We came here by sea, from far away to the south of this great island'.

'What made you come?', we ask. 'Is the south not a warmer, easier place to live?'

'Yes, it is, but at that time there was much fighting in Europe. Tribe against tribe at first, then Roman armies attacking them. Some tribes decided to cross into south Britain. They came in great numbers. Our people built bigger walls round our forts and dug deeper ditches but there was no holding the invaders. They swarmed round our forts, burned down the gates and swept in.' His hand shook on the handle of his iron sword as he remembered. (We call these latest invaders the Belgae from what Julius Caesar wrote about them, but they were Celts too, like the fort peoples they were driving out.)

'You wanted to get away from them', we said.

'Yes, we didn't want them ordering us about. So we loaded up our boats and sailed up here. Our broch is close to the sea.'

'Yes, but the land beside it looks rich too.'

'Yes the cattle are ours', said the old man, 'and we make the farmers here share their grain with us. We are *their* lords.'

We gaze up at the great round tower. It is the tallest building anyone then has ever seen. (The Broch of Mousa in Shetland today is still 13 metres high.) The entrance is low, and blocked by a large stone door. Its stone wall has no weak point on the outside – no openings for windows, for example – and it is far too steep to climb. Light inside comes from above because the broch has no roof on top. It looks a safe place, big, solid and round.

'Was your house in the south a round house?' you ask.

'Yes,' said the old man, 'but it was built of wood, like you will see inside. It is the stone shell that is new. Go in now. My grandson will take you.'

Living in a broch, an artists's view

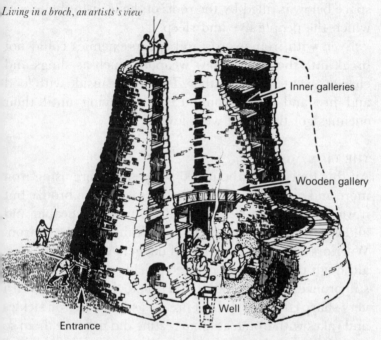

The boy, a sturdy teenager, signs to us to keep our heads down on our way in. On the right he points out the guardroom for armed men defending the entrance. We see a broch really has two walls, an outer and an inner, with a huge gap between them. Soon we are climbing up stone stairs, between the two walls. We stop on a flat floor of big slabs between the walls.

'My grandfather says this open space stops the walls becoming too heavy', said the boy. 'Come on, more stairs to climb!'

47

On top, we meet the boy on look-out duty. Turning to look down inside we can see the fire flaming in the centre and we can smell its woody, peaty smoke. We watch a woman drawing water from a well inside. Most of the space below is filled by the roofs of the lean-to shelters in which the people live and sleep.

Even with iron swords and spears enemies could not break into the broch. New weapons, such as slings and chariots, were no help either. The people inside with food and fire and water could carry on living until their enemies got tired and went away.

THE IRON AGE

All this time, from about 600 BC, people were using iron more and more. It was not a better metal than bronze but it was much easier to produce. This made it cheaper and allowed people to have far more things made of iron. Warriors soon had swords and daggers with iron blades, although their finely decorated shields and sheaths were still bronze. Farmers found that iron tools could be given a very sharp edge and did not break easily. With iron sickles and rakes with iron teeth, harvesting did not take them so long. Woodworkers adopted their own special tools, iron axes, chisels and simple saws, which changed very little in later centuries.

6 In the Time of the Romans

Our visit to the broch people in Chapter 5 taught us that in the first century BC they came as warriors into Scotland and became lords over the native people in the west and north. Invaders who settled south of the Forth found many natives had built defences round their homes, sometimes on the tops of hills, and the invaders did the same.

Two of the hill-forts in the south stand out because they were far bigger than the rest. One was on the North Eildon in Roxburghshire, and the other on Traprain Law, east of Edinburgh. Each covered 16 hectares (about the same as 25 football pitches) and each was the headquarters of a new group of invaders.

The peoples in Scotland were not united. The Romans showed this by giving sixteen names to separate tribes in the country. Round Traprain Law, for example, were the Votadini. West of them round the three Eildon Hills, people were all called Selgovae, whether they were warrior lords or native farmers.

Sometimes a Roman name for a tribe tells us where the new lords came from. The people of Clydesdale were called the Damnonii, for example, very like the Dumnonii in Cornwall and Devon. Another Roman name, Caledonii, at first described one tribe in the Highlands, and later a large group of tribes. It gives us *Caledonia* and the

Caledonians, old names for Scotland and the Scots.

The newcomers were all Celts, who were well known to Roman writers for their love of fighting. They honoured their greatest warriors who became folk heroes, and the *Druids*, who were their priests, had the duty of telling all the stories of the warriors' brave deeds. Like the medicine-men in the stone circles, the Druids were the leaders in the seasonal festivals. The Celts liked to wear bronze armlets and to have finely decorated harness for their horses. They loved to drive into battle in their chariots, shouting challenges and screaming to terrify their enemies.

Modern actors in this photograph give an idea of what Celtic warriors and their chariot probably looked like

NORTH EILDON HILL-FORT

Between AD 43 and AD 80 Roman armies had conquered Britain up to the line between the Solway Firth and the River Tyne. In AD 80 the people on the North Eildon were warned that the Romans were heading their way. Celtic warriors on the run appeared, asking for shelter. 'The Romans are coming', they said, 'thousands and thousands of them.'

They poured out their stories: how the Romans were all trained soldiers, part of a well-run full-time army; how fierce they were in battle; what great defences they put up round their camps, and the catapults they used to knock down other people's. Children shook with fear when they heard how cruel the Romans were in burning forts, homes, crops and taking young people away to be soldiers or slaves. Next day, they saw pillars of smoke rising as settlements they knew went up in flames. Then they spotted the first of the soldiers. On and on they came, marching men and horsemen, more of them and more, so many that they seemed to go on for ever. The people in the fort drove their cattle up inside the fort, closed their gates and waited.

What happened to them, we do not know. The Roman writer, Tacitus, writing about this invasion, says nothing about the Romans having had to fight to take this fort. Hundreds of hut circles can still be seen and prove that there must have been about 2000 people altogether living there. That is a lot, but the number of fighting men they had was low compared with the Roman army advancing on them now. Probably all the Romans had to do was to surround the fort and place their catapults in position. Certainly the Roman general, Agricola, cleared all the Selgovae off the hill. He may also have taken their young men and sent them away to be soldiers in the Roman army across the sea.

Looking for a good position to build a fort, Agricola had found a very good place below the Eildons where he could

The hill-fort on North Eildon in snow, which helps to show up the ditches round it and all the hut circles inside

also build a bridge across the River Tweed. He was too wise to leave Celtic warriors up in a hill-fort where they could sweep down on his men at any time. The great fort he built was a base for both foot-soldiers and cavalry and he called it Trimontium ('Three Mountains') after the three Eildon Hills. Now it is all covered by soil but its outline shows up clearly in the photograph opposite taken from the air. On top of North Eildon Agricola erected one building only. It was a signal station to keep his soldiers in touch with Roman troops in other places.

That is why life in North Eildon hill-fort came to such a sudden end. Craftsmen's tools, found in great numbers when the Roman fort was excavated, are signs of all the skills the Roman soldiers had, besides being fighters. Soldiers, however, have no time to grow their own food.

The farming tools, such as hoes, rakes, sickles, and scythes, which also turned up are more likely to have belonged to native farmers making a living by growing food for the soldiers. Probably they included people who used to live up in the hill-fort.

TRAPRAIN LAW

The Votadini on Traprain Law did not suffer like their neighbours, the Selgovae. Perhaps they quickly offered to help the Romans and be their friends. Perhaps the Romans saw how much this also suited them. All the food and weapons for their soldiers came north by sea. From Traprain Law the Votadini could see the ships and could easily have stopped them unloading. They became the allies, or friends, of the Romans and their settlement on Traprain Law was allowed to grow. Their farmers still

This photograph of the site of the Roman fort at Newstead was taken in July 1977.
Differences of growth in cereal crops pick out details of the site: lines of darker crop follow
the buried remains of the defensive ditches, while paler lines cover the old gravel streets

kept sheep, and their ox-teams ploughed the flat fields below for growing grain. Up on Traprain Law there were people making cloth, others making bronze pins and dress-fasteners, and others glass bangles, which were a Traprain specialty. With these *manufactures* to sell, Traprain became a trading centre, a town on a hill with a wall all round. Roman traders gave Roman pottery, glass and coins in return. From the coins it looks as if trade went on for centuries until about AD 370, as long as any Romans were in Scotland.

THE BATTLE OF MONS GRAUPIUS

Agricola's chief aim was to conquer Scotland, however, not to trade in glass bangles. In AD 84 he pushed north, not into the Highlands but along their eastern edge, building forts as he went. His fort at Inchtuthil on the Tay was big enough to hold 6000 men and there were smaller forts farther north. Somewhere north of Stonehaven (we do not know exactly where), the Caledonian tribes came together under a leader called Calgacus to face Agricola.

Tacitus, Agricola's son-in-law, writes that the two armies met at Mons Graupius, 'Grampian Mountain'. He describes events in the battle: the hand-to-hand fighting with swords, the victory of the Roman cavalry over the Celtic warriors in their chariots, then the mad charge of the Caledonians down the hill, only to be scattered by the Roman cavalry. This was a great Roman victory, but they did not try to conquer the rest of Scotland.

For twenty-five years until AD 105 and again from AD 140 when the Antonine Wall was built, until the end of the century, the line between the Forth and the Clyde was the northern limit of Roman Britain. The rest of the time, until about AD 370, Hadrian's Wall farther south between the Solway and the Tyne was the usual frontier. The Romans did not want the people north of Hadrian's Wall to rise against them, however, and sent cavalry, like the man below, over the Cheviots on patrol from time to time. They were like mounted policemen. They visited hill-forts to see that no one built walls to keep them out. Hut circles down the slope below where the ramparts once had been are signs that Border people must have felt safe enough in houses which did not have defences. Usually, it seems, the Romans were able to keep the peace and keep the natives friendly.

This carving from the Antonine Wall shows what a Roman cavalryman looked like

7 The Picts

In 1969 when a man was making a new garden, his pick struck a large flat stone. When he cleared off the soil he saw that it had mark-
ings on it, a *crescent*
shape with a V cutting
across it, like the draw-
ing on this page. His
nephew who was help-
ing him told one of his
teachers and the stone
was recognised as a Pictish *symbol* stone. Their garden was west of Inverness and very close to the shore of the Beauly Firth.

The stone was said to be 'Pictish' because it was found where the Picts used to live. It is like many other stones which had signs or pictures cut on them in the years after AD 600 when the Picts were known to be there. The crescent and V-rod symbol on the stone is the commonest of all.

A Roman writer called these people *Picti* for the first time in AD 297. The word means 'the painted people'. The Romans used the name to describe all the tribes north of the Forth and Clyde. They were people who had never lived under Roman rule. In the fourth century AD the Picts, as well as the Scots from Ireland, were making raids
56 into Roman Britain. The Picts were not a new people,

however; they were the children of the people in the hill-forts and the brochs, and all the people before them. They occupied the northern two-thirds of the area we now call Scotland.

PICTISH HOMES

Some of the Picts lived on in the hill-top forts. Others built a new kind of fort, called a 'nuclear' fort. Instead of a hill with a flat top, they chose a craggy hill. They tried to use the hill's natural outcrops of rock as defences and built walls to join them up. Their aim was to make each layer of the fort an area they could defend. Enemies would have to fight to capture the lowest part of the fort, and fight all over again to reach the next. The forts were the homes of chiefs, perhaps even of kings. Dunadd in Argyll is a nuclear fort (see page 69), which became the *capital* of the Scots in the sixth and seventh centuries, and the castle rocks of Edinburgh and Stirling were probably once forts.

It is more difficult to find the homes of lowland farmers in the north-east. Several *souterrains*, which means 'houses under the ground', have been discovered in Aberdeenshire and Angus. These made people think that Pictish farmers lived under the ground. Excavations recently, however, have shown that the souterrain was more suited as a cool place for storing food than a home for humans. Beside it there had been round huts with sloping roofs which looked like wigwams. Can you see the outline of one on p. 58? Their floors were paved with stones and their roofs were thatched with bracken and turf. These were the houses the Picts used to live in, on top of the ground.

PUZZLES ABOUT THE PICTS.

When a king dies, his eldest son becomes the next king:

A picture taken from the air at Newmill in Perthshire. The ring of big post-holes (above) shows the shape of a Pictish house and (below) the paved souterrain once had a wooden roof

that was the custom among all the peoples in Europe – except the Picts. Their rule was quite different. A son did not gain the right to be king through his father, but through his mother. His younger brother might succeed him because they had the same mother. The younger brother might in time be succeeded by his sister's son, his nephew, because the right to the throne passed down through the females in the family. This made mothers important in the eyes of the Picts. It did not make them queens, but it made their sons kings. How the Picts alone came to choose their kings this way, we do not know.

Most of us learn two languages, English and French perhaps, or Gaelic and English, or 'classroom' and 'playground', and we know that it is possible to *translate* what somebody said or wrote in one language into another. The broch-builders, coming from south Britain before the Romans invaded, must have spoken the same Celtic language as the Britons. It survives today in modern Welsh. The rest of the Picts, however, spoke Pictish. That is a language which nobody today can read and nobody can translate. It is not like any other language in Europe and must therefore be very old. It could have been the language the earliest farmers spoke. Invaders who came later probably had to learn the native language and gradually gave up their own, if they wanted to talk to the local people or marry the local girls.

The Picts did not write anything on paper. The only signs that they could write are notches they cut on stone with a chisel. The notches make up letters in an early form of alphabet called *ogam* which we know because the Celts also used it. When we learn to write, most of our letters sit on the line while one or two letters, like 'g' and 'p' cross it and continue below the line. Later we can write without lines. However, in ogam the position of the line is very important. Strokes below the line provide five letters: add a stroke and you change the letter each time, like this:

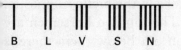

B L V S N

Strokes above the line give another five:

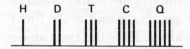

Five other letters extend above and below the line; so do the last five but they lie at an angle:

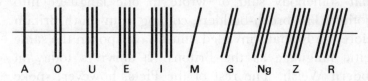

Knowing their alphabet, we can turn their strokes into letters, and their groups of letters into words, but we still cannot tell what the Pictish words mean.

CLUES TO THE PICTS

The homes of the Picts tell us only that they were farming people who liked to have safe places to live in. We know nothing about their home lives, their families, or how they buried people. No Pictish graves have been found so far. When writers in other languages record battles the Picts took part in they are also telling us the Picts were a fighting people. Some pictures Pictish *sculptors* carved on stones also prove that this is true.

For example, a big stone at Aberlemno in Angus was carved about AD 750. The splendid Christian cross on one side reminds us that by then the Picts were Christian. On the other side, which you can see in the picture opposite, the Picts themselves appear. The top two horsemen are charging in the same direction but below them there is clearly a battle. Three foot-soldiers with spears and shields are standing up to a horseman who is charging at them armed with a spear and a round shield. What do you notice about his helmet? At the bottom, soldiers on horseback are about to clash, spear and sword at the ready. On the right, still wearing his helmet and a long shirt or leather coat, is a man who is probably dead or wounded. What do you see attacking him? On another stone, in Easter Ross, which you can see on page 62, we see the Picts out hunting. One of the hunters is a woman riding side-saddle and their long lean hounds are bounding along at speed beside them. These pictures on stones give us interesting glimpses into the lives of the Picts.

The earlier carved stones are simpler and more mysterious. In the V-rod on the stone that the gardeners

The Picts fighting, as shown on the stone found at Aberlemno

Carving on the stones in Easter Ross, showing Picts out hunting

found one end is pointed like the tip of an arrow and the other end is like its flight feathers. Could a V-rod be a broken arrow? Z-shapes are also pointed: could they be broken spears? Other signs include a mirror and comb together, said to stand for a woman. Animals often appear: the bull is common near Burghead in Moray; the wolf and the boar appear, as well as birds, and the salmon only on stones near rivers. Each stone is like a notice-board, but what does it say?

Perhaps the stones show who owns a piece of land and the rights he claims. The crescent and a V-rod, for example, may be a sign for a chief of a certain rank. The same sign with a mirror and comb below it may stand for his widow or his mother. A bull could be the sign of a chief's claim to grazing rights, the wolf and the boar to hunting rights, and the salmon to fishing rights. They could be gravestones, but no human bones have been dug up near them. What do you think? The stones are still an exciting mystery.

The signs on stones in different places look so alike that the same man must have carved a lot of them. The best crescent and V-rod signs appear near Golspie in Sutherland (see drawing on page 56). We can imagine a sculptor and his *apprentice* in a workyard near the shore. Having marked the design on the stone the sculptor cuts the outline by tapping his sharp iron punch with his hammer. The boy smoothes the punch marks with a stone. The sculptor is also teaching him to use the tools and the boy has nearly finished cutting a simple outline of a crescent and V-rod sign all by himself. When they have several stones ready they load them into their boat and take them to people who want them along the coast.

Later a sculptor cut the same designs on stones on the south side of the Moray Firth. It could have been this boy, perhaps called there by a Pictish chief in Aberdeenshire. Certainly someone was working near the great vitrified fort called Tap o' Noth near Rhynie and sending out carved stones in all directions along the river valleys. A ploughman discovered more of this man's work when his plough struck a large buried stone there in 1978. On it was the bold outline of the Pict on the left of page 64, a bearded man with long hair, wearing a short tunic and carrying a   63 long axe in his right hand. He is very like the other carved figure. Look at the direction he is facing, his tunic, his nose and beard, and what he has in his right hand. The similarities make us think there must be a connection between the two, and indeed the second stone was carved by the sculptor at Golspie.

Rhynie man   *Golspie man*

The silver treasure on St Ninian's Isle (page 5) in Shetland has no connection with St Ninian. It is much later and it shows how rich a Pictish chief or a church might be. A silver chain found near the River Ness in 1807 by workmen digging the Caledonian Canal is also Pictish and weighs more than 3 kilos, far too heavy for anyone to wear all day every day. Perhaps some great chief put it on when he was attending the king of the Picts. King Brude, we know, lived in a fortress somewhere above the River Ness, probably on Craig Phadrig.

64

Ninian was the first *missionary* to the Picts. He was a British boy, brought up as a Christian and educated in the Roman church. His first church at Whithorn in Galloway in the south-west of Scotland was built of stone about AD 400 and Bede, the monk of Jarrow, wrote that it was commonly called 'the white house'. The foundations of a very early building, excavated close to Whithorn Priory, did have traces of white plaster on the outside and this may have been his church. Ninian trained missionaries and set off with them to convert the Picts. An early church at Eccles near Stirling which is dedicated to him marked his entry into Pictland. Other churches called 'St Ninian's' occur at Dunottar and Methlick in the north-east, Navidale in Sutherland and St Ninian's Isle in far-off Shetland, but probably Ninian converted the southern Picts only and never travelled so far north.

Columba came later, following other Scots from Ireland who had settled in Argyll. Columba and his twelve companions left Ireland in 563 and landed on the island of Iona. They built a settlement there with a wall all round. There was a church and a separate hut for each monk to sleep in, a kitchen and a place to eat, a workshop and a guest-house for the pilgrims who came to visit them. In Columba's time, they were farmers keeping animals and gardeners growing vegetables. In 1979 archaeologists excavating their workshop discovered that they made their own shoes out of cowhide, turned drinking bowls out of the wood of the alder tree and made their own ink out of holly bark and water. They often left the island to take the message about Jesus to the Picts in the north. We know, for example, that they travelled up the lochs in the Great Glen, including Loch Ness, until they came to king

65

A priest at the altar with the cup and the cross, a scene carved on stone in Iona

Brude's fort. The monk who wrote Columba's life tells the story:

> After the saint's tiring journey the king did not open the gate of his fortress when he arrived. Columba went with his companions up to the doors of the fort, put the sign of the Lord's cross on the doors, then knocked and laid his hand upon them. Immediately the doors flew open by themselves and Columba and his companions went in. Learning this, the king and his council came to meet him and spoke to him very pleasantly with words of peace.

How much this 'miracle' helped it is hard to tell, but king Brude agreed to give his protection to the missionaries, even those working as far away from Iona as Orkney. Another time, Columba met a monster in the River Ness. This terrifying water beast was rushing with its jaws wide open to attack a monk who was swimming across the river. At once Columba made the sign of the cross, ordered the monster to go away and leave the man alone. It obeyed and disappeared immediately. The Picts, we are told, saw this as another sign of the power of God.

8 The Scots and Scotland

From the first visitors to Scotland in 5500 BC to the Picts in AD 500 – 6,000 years of people living in Scotland – we have heard hardly anything about the Scots!

Until the fifth century AD the Scots lived in Ireland. They spoke Gaelic and called themselves Gaels. Roman writers, however, writing about the raids they made on Roman Britain called them 'Scots'. Then some Scots left the north of Ireland and settled on islands such as Islay and Jura and the mainland of Argyll. They called it Dalriada, which means 'kingdom of the Scots', and their king who came over about AD 500 was Fergus *Mor*. Dunadd, the nuclear fort in mid-Argyll, became their capital. These places had belonged to the Picts. The Scots attacked the Picts north of the Forth and the Britons to the south.

But the Scots were not the only enemies the Picts had to face. When the Romans left, the Anglo-Saxons (or English) from Germany invaded Britain. They took over the land and drove the Britons west. One of the new English kingdoms, Northumbria, spread right up to the River Forth and it looked as if the Northumbrians might conquer all the peoples in the north, the Britons, the Picts and the Scots. The Picts under their king Brude, son of Bili, saved them by winning a great victory. This was at the battle of Nectansmere in Angus in AD 685. If Brude's

Dunadd, a nuclear fort in Argyll, which was once the capital of the Scots

men had failed, the English might have gone on and conquered all the Highlands and there would have been no Scotland at all.

In AD 843, however, Kenneth *Mac* Alpin, king of Scots, became king of the Picts as well. By this time both Scots and Picts were Christian and Kenneth may have had a claim to the Pictish throne through his mother. With one king, a Scot, ruling over all the people north of the Forth and Clyde, everyone began to speak Gaelic, the language of the Scots, and the Pictish language died out. The capital of the new kingdom was at Scone, the place where the ceremony of making men kings of Scots was to take place for centuries to come.

The Scots expanded south and took Edinburgh in the next century. In 1018, when their king Malcolm II defeated the English at Carham on the River Tweed, the English-speaking people in Lothian came under the rule 69

The peoples in Scotland who later became the Scots

of the king of Scots and the frontier with England was pushed south to the Tweed. In 1034 Malcolm's grandson, Duncan, succeeded him, and as he was already king of the Britons of Strathclyde, he brought in the whole of the south-west from the Clyde to the Solway Firth. Duncan was the first king of Scots to rule over all the people, except for the Vikings in the far north. The people became the Scots of later history in a country roughly the size and shape Scotland is today.

How do we Know?

In this book you have read about the finds which gardeners, farmers and children have made by chance, and discoveries like the Balbridie house made by the Archaeological Air Survey whose job is to go out and look for ancient sites. The important person in all this is the archaeologist who looks at the clues and takes charge of any excavation. Our best way of learning about early peoples is by reading the reports archaeologists write on what they have found, especially about how people lived. Other experts help. Botanists can tell from looking at pollen samples what trees and plants were growing at a certain time. Geologists can trace where certain stones came from and zoologists can tell what the animal bones are.

If a site has not been excavated completely, like the Ring of Brodgar in Chapter 3, there is much less information to go on. Sometimes we have to use finds from other sites of about the same date. Proof of animal sacrifices, for example, comes from burned bones of sheep, ox and wolf found at the Stones of Stenness close by. We think they painted their bodies because of the paint found at Skara Brae, not far away. Sometimes too we can learn from people abroad, like the Virginian Indians on the next page, who, much closer to our time, were following the same way of life as New Stone Age people here.

From the first century AD when the Romans came, we have a new kind of evidence about early Scotland, written evidence. True, the writers were Roman, writing for Roman readers but sometimes the story they tell fits in well with the other clues archaeologists have found. Sometimes it does not. Does this

These people dancing round a circle of carved wooden posts are not from our New Stone Age but are American Indians in Virginia in the sixteenth century

description sound like what you have learned about the people in Scotland in Roman times?

> They live on rugged hills, with neither walled places, nor towns, nor cultivated land, but by keeping animals, and by hunting and on certain kinds of berries. They live in tents, naked and shoeless.

You can read about the lives of the Romans when they were in Scotland in another Then and There book called 'The Romans in Scotland'.

Visiting archaeological sites can be exciting. Before writing this book, I visited nearly all the settlements, forts, stone circles and tombs mentioned here, from the Cheviots to Orkney and the Isle of Lewis. There are probably several not far from you. Some sites have small museums where you can see the objects found in excavations. Your town museum probably contains most of the archaeological finds made in your area and should be your chief source of information. The National Museum of Antiquities in Edinburgh has a wealth of interesting things found in early Scotland. These will open our eyes to the people of Skara Brae, and the brochs, the Picts, and the treasure the boy found on St Ninian's Isle.

When you visit an early site, respect it because it is an important piece of evidence about the past. Avoid damaging it in any way. And if you should find something which you think is early, treat it with the greatest care. Perhaps the last person who touched it was a Stone Age hunter! Report it to the local museum. If an excavation is decided on you will probably be invited. Then you will see how archaeologists work and add to what we know about early Scotland.

Things To Do

1. Why did the first people at Morton not stay on there?

2. a) What kind of farming was more important at Skara Brae, growing crops or keeping animals?
   b) What other jobs did the people at Skara Brae have?
   c) In what ways were the people of Skara Brae more 'advanced' than the people at Morton?

3. a) Describe, with drawings if possible, how you think the big stones in the Ring of Brodgar got there.
   b) Judging from all the work needed to erect such a stone circle, how important do you think it was in people's lives?

4. Imagine you are helping in the excavation of a broch where the following finds have been made:

   Metal: 1 iron axe, 1 iron spearhead
   Antler: 1 antler pick, worn on the point
   Bone: 1 needle, 1 whalebone comb shaped like a hand, 3 long dice, with numbers,
   Stone: 3 spinning whorls, 2 round flat stones (look up saddle quern in glossary), 1 pebble of quartz with a groove worn across it (look up strike-a-light in glossary).
   Pottery: several pieces from large decorated pots

   Many bones of young cattle, sheep and pigs; some from red deer, whale, seal; some charcoal, much peat ash.

   From this broch write a report on the way of life of the broch people – their work, food, clothes, home, and pastimes. Try to make use of as many of the finds as you can.

5. a) Write an imaginary conversation in which natives of North Eildon and Traprain Law talk about the Romans.

b) Draw a Celtic warrior and a Roman soldier.
   c) Write a play or story about Columba visiting the king of
      the Picts.
6. a) Write a message in ogam, as if it were a secret code.
   b) Try to read someone else's secret message.
7. Copy the table below and try to fill in the missing words. The
   first example has been done for you.

Who?	More recently than in early Scotland	Where?
a) Eskimos	built homes similar to Skara Brae using blocks of ice	Canada
b)	lived in round huts with thatched roofs	
c)	carried homes of poles and skins about with them	
d)	lived in defended homes on mounds or hills	

Make drawings or try to find pictures of these and stick them
in your book.

8. Start a class museum:
   a) Make a map of local settlements and early finds.
   b) Make models or drawings of the settlements, tombs, etc.,
      as they must have been. Polystyrene is an easy material
      for making huts, forts, brochs.
   c) Make copies of finds in the local museum. You can use
      plasticine for flints, stone axeheads and pots, and wood
      painted to look like bronze and iron weapons.
   d) Make a measuring stick 1 MY (0.83 m) long
   e) Make plasticine figures of a man and a woman in the New
      Stone Age and the Bronze Age and dress them in the sort
      of clothes they would have worn.
   f) Make and dress a model of Rhynie man, a Pict.

Glossary

AD, *anno Domini*, in the year (of the birth) of our Lord (Christ)

antler, stag's horn

apprentice, person learning a skill

archaeologist, someone who digs up and studies the things earl people left behind to find out how they lived

ard, light plough which scratched the surface of the soil

astronomer, someone who studies the position of stars and th movement of planets

awl, pointed tool for making little holes

BC, before Christ's birth

beaker, finely made drinking pot, sometimes shaped like a upturned bell

broch, round stone tower

bronze, a metal – a mixture of copper and tin

Caledonia, old name for the Highlands, and later the whole c Scotland

capital, chief town or centre of government

carbon-14 (radiocarbon), the radioactive carbon which exists in all living things

cardinal points, the four chief points of the compass – north south, east, west

causeway, paved way or path

chambered tomb, New Stone Age family burial place built of larg stones and covered in a mound of stones

charcoal, carbon, made by burning wood

chert, hard stone like flint

chocking stone, stone shaped like a wedge, used to keep a standin stone upright *circumference*, line round the outside edge of a circle

cist, short grave lined with stone slabs, used in Beaker times to hold one body

crescent, shape like the moon between new moon and full moon

diameter, distance across a circle through the centre

dike, stone wall round a field

Druids, educated men among the Celts, their priests and story-tellers

excavate, to uncover the remains early people have left behind by digging

flange, raised edge

flax, plant with fibres used to make linen

flint, very hard rock from which early men made tools with sharp edges

flue, opening through which heat or smoke are drawn

gannet, big white sea-bird

glacier, huge mass of ice creeping slowly down a mountain

haft, handle

harpoon, spear with barbs

hoard, hidden store

ingot, lump of unworked metal

jet, hard black stone which can be highly polished, used as jewellery

kiln, very hot oven made of brick, in which pottery is baked

loom, wooden frame on which cloth is woven

mac, son of

manufactures, goods made by hand

megaliths, very large stones

megalithic yard, (MY) unit used by megalithic builders equal to the length of a man's pace and measuring 2 feet 8⅔ inches (0.83 metres)

midden, rubbish heap

missionary, person sent out to preach and convert other people

mor, great or tall

mortar, cement and sand mixed with water and used for building today

mould, hollow in which clay or molten metal takes shape

moulting (of a bird), shedding its feathers

ogam, early alphabet of twenty letters

'*Picti*', 'the painted men', name given by the Romans to the people of the north

radius, distance from the centre to the rim of a circle

rampart, high broad wall of earth built to fortify a camp

sacrifice, offering to the gods

saddle quern, stone low in the centre on which grain was ground into flour

sculptor, someone who carves figures on or out of stone

sheerlegs, two tree-trunks with ropes attached, used for lifting things, like an early kind of crane

sinews, muscles

souterrain, underground shelter in Pictland, now thought to be for storing milk and butter

spindle, wooden stick for spinning thread

spiral, something which coils outwards from a central point

strike-a-light, flint or iron striker and a quartz pebble, used for starting a fire

sturgeon, large fish which provides caviar

symbol, sign which stands for something

translate, to put into the words of a different language

vault, roof built like an arch

Vikings, people from Norway who came to Britain in about AD 800 in search of land and treasure

vitrified (of stones), heated until they have melted and joined together and then cooled to form a very hard mass

warp, threads running up and down a piece of cloth

wattle and daub, framework of interwoven sticks plastered with mud to make a wall, fences etc.

weft, threads which cross and weave in and out of the warp threads

whorl, clay weight on the end of a spindle for spinning

yarn, spun thread

Index

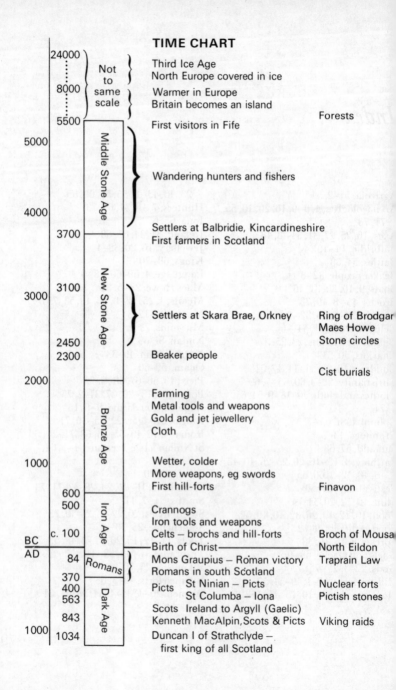

TIME CHART

24000	Not to same scale	Third Ice Age North Europe covered in ice	
8000		Warmer in Europe Britain becomes an island	
5500		First visitors in Fife	Forests
5000	Middle Stone Age	Wandering hunters and fishers	
4000			
3700		Settlers at Balbridie, Kincardineshire First farmers in Scotland	
3100	New Stone Age		
3000		Settlers at Skara Brae, Orkney	Ring of Brodgar Maes Howe Stone circles
2450			
2300		Beaker people	Cist burials
2000	Bronze Age	Farming Metal tools and weapons Gold and jet jewellery Cloth	
1000		Wetter, colder More weapons, eg swords First hill-forts	Finavon
600	Iron Age		
500		Crannogs Iron tools and weapons	
c. 100		Celts – brochs and hill-forts	Broch of Mousa
BC / AD		Birth of Christ	North Eildon
84	Romans	Mons Graupius – Roman victory	Traprain Law
370		Romans in south Scotland	
400	Dark Age	Picts St Ninian – Picts	Nuclear forts
563		St Columba – Iona	Pictish stones
843		Scots Ireland to Argyll (Gaelic) Kenneth MacAlpin, Scots & Picts	Viking raids
1000			
1034		Duncan I of Strathclyde – first king of all Scotland	